Silas Weir Mitchell

The Cup of Youth

And Other Poems

Silas Weir Mitchell

The Cup of Youth
And Other Poems

ISBN/EAN: 9783744710299

Printed in Europe, USA, Canada, Australia, Japan

Cover: Foto ©Thomas Meinert / pixelio.de

More available books at **www.hansebooks.com**

THE CUP OF YOUTH
AND OTHER POEMS

BY

S. WEIR MITCHELL, M.D., LL.D., *Harv.*

AUTHOR OF "THE HILL OF STONES AND OTHER POEMS," "A MASQUE
AND OTHER POEMS"

BOSTON AND NEW YORK
HOUGHTON, MIFFLIN AND COMPANY
The Riverside Press, Cambridge
1889

Dedicatory Epistle

TO

OLIVER WENDELL HOLMES

Dear Doctor:

When I was a young man your kindly advice kept me from inflicting a volume of verse on the public, by which it would not have been profited, and by which I should assuredly have been injured.

Accept this dedication as in some shape the expression of my thanks for that valuable service, which, with the many other kindnesses I owe to your friendship, has no doubt long since slipped out of your memory.

With constant esteem,

Your friend,

THE AUTHOR

CONTENTS.

———✦———

THE CUP OF YOUTH.

———◆———

SCENE, A SEA BEACH NEAR RAVENNA. MOON-
LIGHT.

DRAMATIS PERSONÆ.

GASPAR.	GELOSA, *his wife.*
UBERTO.	EMILIA, *his wife.*
GALILEO.	

TIME, *circa* 1632.

SCENE I. *Gaspar and Gelosa. Gelosa playing with the
sand.*

GASPAR.

Time stays a prisoner in those pretty hands
And all the world stands still for you and me,
Yet must I break the spell and hustle in
The rough world's business. Wherefore, little one,
This long delay? You lacked not courage once.

GELOSA.

Still am I in the bondage of my youth ;
What wonder if the woman find it hard

1

To cast aside the lessons of the child?
All my life long I feared that silent man
Who came across the garden from the tower,
Ate, slept, or to and fro athwart the grass
Trod one same path with bended head and back,
And kept no company with this lower world.
To her who loved him as the worst are loved
But by the best of those who love the best,
Whose love he wasted and whose gold he spent,
Few words he cast, and bitter : but for her
I had not cared to see his face again.

GASPAR.

Men say his silence guards such fateful power
As makes yon stars the vassals of his will,
Turns baser metals into golden coin,
And wrings all secrets from the miser Time.

GELOSA.

And yet he knew not that one summer night
A little maid — Gelosa was her name —
Had stolen out beneath his starry slaves
To learn the subtle alchemy of love
That turns all fates to gold, nor lacks the power
To prophesy the sweetness of to-morrow.
Methinks he knew but little, knowing not
What love will dare ; or haply knew too much
For all the gentler uses of the world
When, like a landlord with too full an inn,

He thrust out Love that ever might have been
The fairest guest his learning entertained.

GASPAR.

Nor I more welcome. I could laugh to think
How patiently I took the beggar's 'Nay'
He cast in scorn. "What! wed a landless squire,
Who spends in folly what he won in blood! —
None but a scholar wins my niece's lands."

GELOSA.

My lands indeed, and if all tales be true,
He married them these many years ago.

GASPAR.

Ay, and may keep them if he be but wise.
Fair over Arno tower my castle walls,
With vine-clad hillsides rolling to the plain.
Nothing I owe you save your own sweet self.
A scholar, I ! Not troubled will you be
By reason of my studies. I shall learn
Love from your eyes ; your lips shall be my law,
And if their ripe decisions please me not,
The fount of justice at its very source
I shall know how to bribe. I brought you here
Because you willed it, — ay, and save for that
I care but little how this errand thrives.

GELOSA.

Kiss me the thoughts away that trouble me ;
The lapsing days will bring some pleasant chance.

GASPAR.

Who trusts a multitude of counselors
Wins sad unrest.

GELOSA.

         Oh, let my mission wait.
How very silent is the sea to-night !
The little waves climb up the shore and lay
Cool cheeks upon the ever-moving sands
That follow swift their whispering retreat.
I would I knew what things their busy tongues
Confess to earth.

GASPAR.

         Let me confess you rather !
Tell me again you love me.

GELOSA.

         Small my need.
'T is in my eyes ; 't is on my lips ; my heart
Beats to this music all **the** long day through.
I am like a bird that hath one only note
For song, for prayer, for thanks, for everything.

GASPAR.

You cannot know how passing sweet it is
To change the camp, the field, the storms of war,
For this and you ; to watch the gray moon wane
And see the slumbrous sea leap here and there
To silver dreams.

GELOSA.

              The hand of time seems stayed,
And joy to own the ever constant hours
So full of still assurance is the night.
Love hath the quiet certainty of heaven,
Rich with the promise of unchanging years.

                      [Voices are heard near by.

GASPAR.

Hush, my Gelosa !   Who be these that come?

Enter Galileo and Uberto, who sit down among the dunes close by.

GELOSA (*aside*).

My uncle and his friend, the Florentine.

GASPAR.

Hark you, he speaks your name. He said, "Gelosa."
He called you — was it Gelosetta, love ?
Why, I shall call you Gelosetta too.

GELOSA.

Distance and absence kept him this one friend,
A scholar, grave and gentle as the gentlest.

GASPAR.

And that is Galileo !　I recall
One day in Florence walking with the Duke,
A man most curious of his fellow-men,
We saw this student wandering to and fro
Intent of gaze where Giotto's campanile
Athwart the plaza sends its shaft of shade.
The Duke had speech with him.　A serious face,
With eyes that seemed to search beyond the earth,
Large, open, peaceful as Luini's saints.

GELOSA.

More sweet than mine ?

GASPAR.

　　　　　　I 'll tell you when 't is **day.**
A mighty student of bright eyes am I ;
Now there I 'll match my science with the best.
Those Florentines, who never want for wit
To label love or hate, say he 's moon-mad,
And hath for mistresses the starry host
That wink at him by night.

GELOSA.

　　　　　　Not Solomon
Had half so many.　Yet for earthlier loves
He lacks not time nor honest appetite ;
He never starved his heart to feed his head.
Hush ! now he speaks again.　The time may serve
To learn my uncle's mood.

GALILEO.

    Your Gelosetta —

UBERTO.

Not ever greatly mine. The wayward child
Grew to the willful woman, ignorant,
Untrained, and wild, a dreamer by the sea, —
Nor hers the housewife's knowledge. I have lived
Companionless of nobler intercourse, —
As to a friend I speak, — my wife wrapped up
In household cares and tendance of the poor,
Death busy with my manhood's friends. I tread
An ever lonelier road.

GALILEO.

    So seem all ways
To him who, yearning for too distant good,
Sees not the sweetness of the common path.
Life hath two hands for those who fitly live:
With one it gives, with one it takes away ;
The willing palm still finds the touch of love,
And he alone has lost the art to live
Who cannot win new friends. Unwise is he
Who scorns the large relationship of life.
Yon restless sea, the sky, the bird, the flower,
The laugh of folly, and the ways of men,
The woman's smile, the hours of idleness,
The court, the street, the busy market-place, —
All that the skies can teach, the earth reveal, —

Are wisdom's bread.   Alas ! the common world
Hath lessons no philosophy can spare ;
The tree that ever spreads its leaves to heaven
Casts equal anchors 'neath the soil below.
The food of life is large, — nay, infinite.
With man it is as with the world he treads :
No little stone of yonder pebbled beach
Could cease to be, and this great rolling orb
Feel not its loss. Enough of this to-night.
Count me your gains a little.   Years have gone
Since last we met : what good thing have they brought?

UBERTO.

To-morrow I will tell you.   Now to-night
My mind is ill at ease ; come, let us go,
But, as my love is valued by your own,
Speak not again of that unthankful child.

GALILEO.

And yet I loved her.   Have it as you will.

> [*Exit Galileo and* Uberto.

GELOSA.

O Gaspar, said I not that age was cruel ?
Be but your youth as kind.

GASPAR.

                    And I could thank
The misery that doubly sweetens love.

Strange seemed my life to him.   To me, as strange
This corner-pickled shrivel of a man,
That all things dreaming never waked enough
To win the sanity of open eyes.
One day in Rimini, before a mirror,
I stood so near my breath the image blurred.
Duke Francis, o'er my shoulder gazing, laughed,
Said I was like some men he knew, and went
And would not read the riddle.   Now 't is clear.
The man that hath no mirror save himself
Blurs the clear image conscience shows us all.
Now for a schoolless, helmet-dinted head,
The guess is not so bad. — What, tears again?
Tears for this man who in your childhood scorned
Its glad prerogatives of love and trust?
A thoughtless falcon, bold and wild of wing,
Like to my lover-self, had better kept
God's pledge to childhood.

GELOSA.

                           Nay, no tears have I
For him who cost me many.   But for her,
The simple, kindly dame who had no will
That was not his, — I am more sad for her,
Because she never learned the woman's art
To traffic with her sadness.   Yet had she
A childless youth ; the children of old age,
Love, solace, cheerful days of quietness
Dead as the little ones she never knew.

Though **sad at best the** husbandry of **years,**
Time in the happy face no furrow **cuts**
That is not wholesome ; but a loveless life,
Sorrow unshared, neglect and lonely hours
Make records sore with shame as are the **scars**
A master's whip leaves to the beaten slave.
Has life no answering scourge for them that sin ?

GASPAR.

For less than this, ay, for **a** moment's wrong
I have **seen** men die young.

GELOSA.

            Let us **go too.**
The night has lost its grace. These memories
Serve but to stir dead hates. To bed, — to bed.
Like his, my mind is very ill at ease ;
I would his hurt were equal to my own.

SCENE II. *Garden of a villa near the sea and border-
ing on a road. Enter Uberto, and walks to and fro.*

UBERTO.

For gain, for lands, for every bribe of power
The soldier wastes the substance of the poor,
Sets ravage free and spills the blood of babes,

THE CUP OF YOUTH.

Yet sleeps as soundly.   Shall I hesitate,
Checked by the memory of an outworn love,
A thoughtless woman and a foolish girl ?
My friend — but he has won the laurel crown.
Dim continents of thought before me lie,
Their harvests wait the vigour of the scythe,
While in my heart the tardy blood of age
Unequal throbs.   The mind, as tremulous
As these thin hands, has lost its certain grasp ;
Pass, ye weak phantasies that bar my way, —
Children of habit, — I will do this thing !

Enter Emilia.

EMILIA (*aside*).

Now help me, Mary Mother, in my need.
Perhaps some memory of our joyous youth —

UBERTO.

What, not abed ?

EMILIA.

        I cannot sleep of late.
As if life were not long enough, the day
Lives through the night, and mocks with time's ex-
    cess.

UBERTO.

Why vex my soul with that of which each hour
Tells the sad tale ?

EMILIA.

   Let us forget, Uberto !
Just half a century gone, when you **and I,**
Just fifty years ago this very night,
Walked 'neath the flowering locust, how I blessed
The kindly shade that hid my blushing cheeks !
Not redder was the moon that night of May.

UBERTO.

Still shall it mock the cheek of other loves
When you and I are gone. **Oh, cruel** time !
You lost the plaything **of a pretty face ; —**
What was your loss **to** mine ? What comfort lies
In useless babble o'er a golden past ?
Lo, when the eager spirit, worn with toil,
Has gathered knowledge, won its lordliest growth,
This robber comes to plunder memory
And lash with needless anguish to the grave.
We scorn the miser who in death laments
The gold he cannot carry ; let us jest
At him whose usury of knowledge stops.

EMILIA.

How know you that it doth ? **To me it seems**
As if no office of our mortal frame
Has more **the signet of** immortal **use**
Than just this common gift of **memory.**
Forgive the thoughts that come I know not whence, —
I think our Galileo said it once, —

The ghosts that haunt the peaceful hours of night
Are not more unaccountable of man
Than the dead thoughts of life that, at a touch,
A taste, an odour, rise, we know not whence,
To scare us with the unforgotten past.
Your knowledge is not like the miser's gold,
For this world's usage only. Yet, perchance,
'T is like in this, that what it was on earth,
Self-ful, or helpful of another's pain,
May set what interest on that gathered hoard
The soul falls heir to in a world to come.

UBERTO.

Alas, were I but sure that after death
I still should carry all life's nobler seed
To ripen largely under other skies
I should not mourn at death.

EMILIA.

Why is it, friend,
That I, for whom this life so little holds,
Should in its cup of emptied sweetness find
The pearl content, and with clear vision see
The stir of angel wings 'neath death's black cloak?
And life, ah, life might still be sweet to me!
O husband, had you been as some have been,
We should have lived a length of tranquil days,
With love slow moving through its autumn-time
To merge in loving friendship, and at last

To find the sainted calm of patient **age,**
Peaceful and passionless, and so have walked
Like little children through life's **wintry ways**
To meet what fate the kindly years decreed. ‖

UBERTO.

Alas, the best is ever to be won !
There is no rose but might have been more red,
There is no fruit might not have been more sweet,
There is **no** sight **so clear but** sadly serves
To set the far horizon farther still.

[*Voices are heard on the road back of them.*

EMILIA (*aside*).

Heart of my hearts !   It is the little one !
My Gelosetta !   Will he know the voice ?

GELOSA (*on the road as she goes by with Gaspar*).

Can the rose-bud ever know
Half how red the rose will grow?
Can the May-day ever guess
Half the summer's loveliness ?

UBERTO.

What voice is that ?

EMILIA.
Some lated village-girl.

UBERTO.

No, 't was Gelosa's.

EMILIA.

Would indeed it were !
Ah, that were joy !   Alas, 't is but the girl
I helped last winter, one the plague cast out
With other Florentines.

[*Aside.*] Would I could see her !

UBERTO.

Come back again to drain our meagre purse.
Ay, there 's the man, — a woman and a man.

A man's voice sings.

'T is better to guess than to see,
'T is better to dream than to be.
The best of life's loving
Is lost in the proving,
'T is better to dream than to be.
The joy of love's sweetness
Is lost with completeness,
'T is better to dream than to be.

EMILIA.

A pair of lovers !   She has found her mate.

UBERTO.

Already doth your cynic lover sing
The death and funeral of love and trust.

Thrice happy **these** with wingless instincts born.
Perhaps is best the woman's ordered life,
Market and house, the husband and the child.

EMILIA.

Mother of God ! and I that have no child !

UBERTO.

St. Margaret I but you women folk are tender.
Enter behind a hedge Gaspar and Gelosa, while Uberto continues.
Forget my haste, Emilia ; **all my** mind
Dwells on the nearness **of one** fateful **hour.**

EMILIA.

Ever the dream that through the weary years
Has turned your life from God, and home, and
        me, —
To win for you that doubtful cup of youth.
Think yet, Uberto, on the thing you do ;
It cannot be that I, grown drear and old,
The very deathtide oozing round my feet,
Shall see you glad and young.   It cannot be
Earth holds **for** me that agonizing hour.
                    [*Uberto rests silent.*

GASPAR.

No answer hath he.   Now speak you to him.
It seems the **wise** man hath no wiser dreams
Than fools are heir to.

GELOSA.

Heard you all he said?

GASPAR.

Ay, all I cared to hear.   Come, let us go.
Seek you his wife alone.   Forget this fool.

GELOSA.

Didst hear, my Gaspar?   Can it be he owns
A cup which drained shall fetch his youth again?
Men say the thing has been in other days.
To leave her old and withered were to add
A crime, unthought of yet, to sin's dark list.

GASPAR.

Less base it were to stab her where she stands.

[*Exit Emilia silently.*

GELOSA.

Hush! she has left him, — left him.   Were I she,
I would crawl out at midnight to his tower.
Deep would I drain the damnèd cup of life,
And wander back a maiden fair and young,
To curse his age with jealous misery.
Or I would kill him as he lay asleep,
And keep him old forever.

2

GASPAR.

Now here 's a wicked lady.   Should I chance
To fall in love with larger length of days,
I should be very careful of my diet.
Comes now the Florentine.   The play were good,
Were you not in the plot.   They say in Florence
The Pope will have it that this man of stars
Shall spread no gossip as to worlds that roll,
Nor play at Joshua with the Emperor Sun.
To be so wise that all the world 's a fool
Might breed uneasy life.

GELOSA.

                              Perhaps ;   **and** yet, —
You know we little women will have thoughts, —
I was but thinking that to surely own
A soul for actions great beyond compare,
A mind for thoughts that have the native flight
Of eaglets rising from the parent nest,
To soar so high they cast no earthward shade,
Why, that might bring a childhood of content,
Should smile as sweetly at the babbling crowd
As though it cheered him with the tongues of
    heaven.

GASPAR.

There 's ever music in your Umbrian heart
That lived where Dante died.   Yet vain the thought ;
For me the world may skip, or stop, or turn
Back somersaults as likes the blessed Pope.

Where gat you, love, these riddles of the brain,
These comments on a world you never knew?

GELOSA.

A certain soldier taught me.   Ah, you smile!
To greatly love is to be greatly wise.
God were less wise were He not also love.
Ah, there 's a riddle only love can read!

Enter Galileo to Uberto, still seated.

GALILEO.

Far have I sought you through the ilex grove,
Among Emilia's roses, in your tower.

UBERTO.

My tower — you saw —

GALILEO.

Saw nothing.   [*Aside.*] He distrusts me.

UBERTO.

Forgive me.   You shall see, shall hear, to-night.

GALILEO.

Those many years since I, a jocund lad,
To you, my elder, turned for counsel, help,
Came back to me to-day.   You were more kind
Than brothers are.   Ah, happy, studious hours!

What **was** the Pope to me, or I to him?
A Cardinal was as the farthest star,
Outside the orbit of my hopes and fears.
I came to you to share some idle days,
To get again within your life of thought,
To question and be questioned.

UBERTO.

Wherefore not?

GALILEO.

A messenger who followed me with haste
Bids me to Rome to answer as I may.
My sin you know.[1]

UBERTO.

What answer can you make?

GALILEO.

Alas, it moves! This ever-patient globe
Moves, with the Pope and me, would move without.
Could I but summon God to answer them!
If He has whispered in my listening ear
This secret, guarded since the morn of time,
How shall I say I know not it nor Him?
A man may love or not, rejoice or not,
Do or do not, but what he thinks is sped;
These word-winged arrows have eternal flight.

UBERTO.

But you, the archer, you who loosed the string,
What harm if you should say this was not yours?—
This troubling doctrine long ago was born;
Sages in Egypt knew it. Or, at need,
Say that the world is stiller than a snail.
Say what you will, but live **to draw anew**
That bow of thought which you alone can draw.

GALILEO.

Death is more wise than any wisest thought
The living man can think; death is more great
Than any life; and as for that stern hour
I meet in Rome next week, **I** know not now
How I shall judge my judge.

UBERTO.

              The fate I fear,
I fear for you, but would not for myself.
Ay, at this hour would I change lives with you;
For come what may, chains, prison, rack, or axe,
You will have lived so largely that no fate
Can pain your age with sense of unfulfilment.
But I have all things willed, yet nothing done.

GALILEO.

I cannot think your solitary years
Have won us nothing, as you seem to say.
And now my hours are **few.** I go to-morrow

Perhaps no **more to** hear a friendly voice,
Or guess the starry secrets of the night.

UBERTO.

Be patient with me.   Many a year ago,
At twilight walking by the darkened sea,
The sudden glory of a broadening thought
Smote me with light as if through doors cast wide
To one **in** darkness prisoned.   Then I saw
Dimly, **as if at dusk,** vast open **space**
Of things long guessed, **but waiting fuller** light.
What could I but despair ?   **The hand and** brain
No longer did my errands.   **There was set**
A task for youth and vigour.   Steadily
I gave my age to win the gift of youth,
That youth might help my quest.

                    That charm I sought
Which vexed the soul of old philosophy.
I won it, friend !   To-night I drain this cup.
Like autumn leaves the withered years shall fall,
And sudden spring be mine.   With wisdom clad,
With knowledge, not of youth, assured of time,
I shall speed swiftly to my certain goal.
The midnight calls my steps to yonder tower,
Where youth, the bride, awaits my joy's delay.
You have **my secret.**

GALILEO.

            In this weary search
Great minds have perished. Where you think to
    win, —
In this the masters failed. Their wrecks of thought
Are in great volumes scattered. Yet it may be.
The strange is only what has never been,
And every century gives the last the lie.
But if 't is so, there 's that within your cup
Might stay the wiser hand. Ay, if 't is so !

UBERTO.

If ? if 't is so ? It is ! Not vain the work
That filled these longing years. For no base end
These wasting vigils and these anxious days.
The gains I win shall lessen human pain.
One re-created life to man shall bring
Uncounted centuries in the gathering sum.

GALILEO.

I neither doubt the harvest nor the power
To reap its glorious fruit. And yet — and yet —
If the strong river of your flowing life
You shall turn back to be again the brook,
Is 't natural to think 't will float great ships,
Or with its lessened vigour roll the mill ?
I too am of that sacred guild whose creed,
Before Christ died or Luke the healer lived,
Taught temperance, honour, chastity, and love.

Enough of me. I go to meet my fate.
Would I could stay !

UBERTO.

           Ah ! when in Pisa's dome
You watched the lamp swing constant in its arc,
You gave to man another punctual slave,
And bade it time for us the throbbing pulse ;[2]
Joyful I guessed the gain for art and life.
Not that frail English boy Fabricius taught,
Not sad Servetus, **nor that daring soul,**
Our brave Vesalius, **e'er had matched your power**
To read the riddles of this **mortal frame.**
And then you left us. Would our strange machine
Had kept your toil, and cheated yon fair stars !

GALILEO.

We do but what we must. Some instinct guides.
To-night, when all the morrow world seems dim
And life itself a thing of numbered hours,
With clearing vision still for you I doubt.
Life hath its despot laws. You more than I
Know all their tyrant rigour. Tempt it not,
Lest failure, anguish, lurk within the cup.
Think sanely of this venture ; let it pass.
Fill full, God helping, all the years He leaves.
Set 'gainst the darkness of death's nearing hour
In wholesome light all human action shines.
This dream is childlike ; you will wake to tears.

Ask of your life if you have life deserved.
What did you with the gift?   You had of it
All that another hath, or long or short.
Not time, but action, is the clock of man.
I should go happier hence if I could set
Your fatal cup aside. Nay, sorrow not ;
Thank God for me.   I have not vainly lived.
The joy to know they cannot rob me of.
Truth have I served, and God, in serving her :
That heritage is deathless as Himself.
Something the thinker of the poet hath ;
Our Dante was no mean philosopher.
With prophet eyes I see a freer day,
When thought shall mock at Kaiser and at Pope.
How can they think to chain this viewless thing,
Which is a very life within the life,
And in the irresponsible hours of sleep
Brings thought unto fruition ?   Yea, ethereal !
Of all God's mysteries most near to Him ;
Instinctively creative, like the woman
Pledged by conception's joy to labour's toil.
Grieve not for me.   All that is best shall live.
There is no rack for thought ; no axe, no block,
Can silence that.

UBERTO.

         But what, dear friend, if I
Should bid you laugh at Pope or Cardinal ?
Take you this cup of mine.   Take it and live.
In youth's disguise lie safety, freedom, life.

GALILEO (*aside*).

Not stranger in its orbit moves **my** world
Than man, its habitant. Why, here is one
Could squander years and cheat a woman's love,
Yet turn to offer this.   Not I, indeed !
[*Aloud.*] Life has been very dear to me, Uberto,
For that it has and that it has not been.
How many in their tender multitude
The cobweb ties of friendship, labour, love,
I knew not till this cruel storm of fate
Did thread them thick with jewels numberless.
And yet life owns no bribe **would bid me back**
To live it o'er anew.   I can but thank you.

UBERTO.

Is **it only they** who have no life of worth
Crave leave **to live** again ?

GALILEO.

That is not all.
Vainly and long would we have talked of it
In other days.   No life is what it seems.
If thought were man's whole company in life,
Who would not live it o'er ?   But by our side
Friends, comrades, walk and torture us with loss.
Who is there born would will to **live** again
Such anguish **as the** happiest have known?
This is the heart's half only ; more there is.
But the night **wastes.**   [*Rises.*

UBERTO.

        To-morrow you go hence?
Write me from Rome. Before the day is spent
I shall have won or lost. Good-night, good friend.
                           [Exit both.

GASPAR.

These learned folks are not more gay to hear
Than Lenten priests. I gave their riddles up
This half hour since. And you?

GELOSA.

               I heard it all.
Love, friendship, reason, all alike are vain.

GASPAR.

Had I a minute in his secret den,
That draught of his should give eternal life
To the foul weeds that rot around the moat.
                   [Gelosa whispers.
The jest were good. Is there no peril in it?

GELOSA.

None, Gaspar. Wait for me beside the gate.
Quick, ere the chance be lost! 'T is past eleven.
Oh, he will like my jest. Come, this way, come!

SCENE III. *Stairway of the* **tower**, *where Emilia sits weeping at the door of the astrologer's laboratory; a small lamp beside her.*

EMILIA.

Though he should kill me I will wait for him.
To die were easy, if to die would stay
His hand from **wrong**.   Alas! **too sure it is,**
Living or dead, I nothing am **to him.**
Who is it comes?   Say, is it **you, Uberto?**

Gelosa **comes up the** *stairs.*

GELOSA.

Oh, mother, it is I, your little one!
Friends, husband, wealth, all that life hath to give,
Are mine to-day.   Come to my Tuscan home.
The flowers you love watch for you on the hills.
My children shall be yours.   My good lord waits
Our coming at the gate.   Leave this old man.

EMILIA.

I cannot, child.

GELOSA.

Then must I talk with him.

For this we came from Florence.   Once again,
I must be sure his will is as of old.

EMILIA.

Vain is your errand, child.

GELOSA.

Yet shall I try ;
[*Aside.*] The equal years give me at last my turn.
[*Aloud.*] Is the door barred?

EMILIA.

Nay, but I dare not enter.

GELOSA.

Not long the thing you fear shall vex your soul.
Come with me.   Spill the cursèd cup, or wreck
With wholesome fire this chamber of your fear.

EMILIA.

Who has betrayed his secrets?

GELOSA.

He himself.
Hid by the ilex hedge I heard it all.
Wept with you, for you; heard your tender plea.
Of other make am I.   Give me your ring.
You used to say I had your sister's voice,
Twin to your own.

EMILIA.

What would you say to him?
What do to him?   You cannot mean him ill.

GELOSA.

Not I, indeed.   **Hark!** there's a voice without.
Trust me a little.   Quick! the ring, the ring!
No other hope is left.   Give me the ring!

EMILIA.

You will not harm him?   I shall have it back?
He gave it me the day we were betrothed.

GELOSA.

A goodly **half of this world's misery**
Is born **of woman's patience.   Could** you live
From that to this?

EMILIA.

                What can a woman else?

GELOSA.

What else? Naught now. The ring, and have no fear!
    [*Takes her hand and removes the emerald ring, which is
      yielded reluctantly.*
Alas, poor withered hand! **how** dear thou art,
And sweet with use of bounty!
                              Quick, the lamp:
And wait for me **upon the** upper stair.
                              [*Urges her hastily*

EMILIA.

Nay, tell me more.   I am afraid, Gelosa.

GELOSA.

Of me who love you?   There, a kiss ; good-by.
And stir not, if you love or him or me.

[*Gelosa opens the door, and with the lamp in **her hand** enters the room.   Emilia ascends the upper staircase.*]

There may be too much sweetness in a woman.
A little **sour** upon the shadowed side
My Tuscan peaches have.

Sweet Mary, what a den !
A winter wealth of kindling in old books.
Bones, — that 's not pleasant.   Vipers, slimy things.
A crocodile that hath an evil eye.   [*Crosses herself.*]
And dust, ye Saints ! but here 's a long day's work.

[*Lifts a bell glass **from a small Venice** goblet containing a transparent fluid.*]

Around the rim twin serpents writhe in coils.

[*Reads the **inscription below** them.*]

Ex morte vitam.   Life is child of death.
This must be it, — the draught to make **man young** :
Now should I drink it, 't were a merry jest,
To find **myself a baby tumbling** round,
Hungry for mother's milk.   Not I, indeed.

[*Empties **cup** on the floor, and refills it with water.   Blows out the light and veils herself.*]

The moon is quite enough.   Will he be long ?
Now, kindly uncle, for this pretty play.

[*She conceals herself in a corner.   Enter **Uberto.***]

UBERTO.

At last, 'tis near. The stairs my constant feet
Have worn with many steps more toilsome grow.
The hounds of time are on their panting prey;
I wait no longer. No man owns to-morrow.
To-morrow is the fool's to-day. Ah, soon
I shall go gaily tripping down the hill,
Glad as a springtide swallow on the wing,
A man new born. **Yes, this** is nearest death.
Why should I falter **here?** We both are old.
Soon in **the common way our** steps would part.
And to be young; to **feel the sinews** supple,
Eye, ear, and motion quick, **the brain all** life, —
The visions of my manhood round me whirl,
White limbs, red lips, and love's delirious dream,
The passion kiss of wine, **the** idle hours
Unmissed from youth's abounding heritage.
Off, off, ye brutal years that gnaw our age!
Come, joy! come, life! — life at the full of flood!
What wonder that my head swims dizzily?

                                         [*Pauses.*

Birth is not ours. **We are,** and that is all.
Death is not ours. We die, and that is all.
This stranger birth that waits my trembling grasp, —
Ay, this is mine alone. The herd of men
Are born and die.   [*Takes the hour-glass.*

                This none can share with me.
The silent planets shine upon the hour.
Swift waste the sands. So much of age is **left.**

Uncounted memories of things long lost
Leap to my view, as if to one who stands
Beside the waif-thronged surges of the deep,
And sees its dead roll passive to his feet,
Its pearls, its weeds, its wrecks.

So let it end.

[*Fills up the glass with wine.*

Nor fear, nor friend, nor love shall hinder me.

[*Drinks.*

Will it be swift? or will the change be like
The wonder work of spring?

[*Lights a small lamp, and examines his face in a mirror.*

A ghastly face!

Is this the earthquake agony of change?

[*Gelosa, still veiled, advances.*

GELOSA.

Change that will never come.   You that would cheat
A life-worn love of company to death,
Take the stern answer of her tortured soul.
You drained my cup of life, and cast aside
The poor mean vessel.   I, Emilia, stole
Your cup of life.   Mine is the youth you craved,
Mine the gay dream of girlhood's rosy joy,
Mine once again the wooing lips you kissed
When you and I were young.   Ah, sweet is youth !
Go, thieving dotard, to a loveless grave !

[*Uberto staggers forward, with the lamp in his hand.*

3

UBERTO.

My wife, Emilia?   No, no, not Emilia.

GELOSA.

Nay, touch me not!   And is your memory dead?
Why, even I some dim remembrance keep.
Take back this ring, this pledge of endless love.

> *[Uberto receives it.*

UBERTO.

Her ring — your ring — Emilia! — **Lost,** lost, lost!
Life, honour, fame, and youth.   **Emilia, wife,**
Speak kindlier to me.   Speak, oh, **speak** again!
Your voice is like an echo from the past. —
What devil taught **you this?**   *[Advances.*

GELOSA.

                    Off, off, old man!
What has a girl to do with palsied age?
I 'll **be a** daughter to your feebleness,
And fetch your crutch, and set you in the sun,
And get me lovers kin to me in years.

UBERTO.

Black Satan take **your** kindness!   Yet have **I**
The strength to kill you!   **You** shall die for this!

> *[Seizes her.*

GELOSA.

What? — feeble fool!   *[Pushes him away; he falls.*

UBERTO.

This is not my Emilia.
Help, help, without there! Help!

GELOSA.

Come in, — come in!
Well have I fooled a fool with foolishness.

Emilia enters.

EMILIA.

Ill have you done, and cruel I have been.
Oh, you have slain my love!

GELOSA.

Not I, in truth.

UBERTO.

Out, lying baggage! Now I know you well.

GELOSA.

Come you with me, dear mother of my love.
Leave we this base old man. My husband waits.

EMILIA.

Get hence! I never loved you. He knew best.
Pray God I see no more the wicked face
That cheated him and me. Begone, I say!

[*Exit Gelosa.*

THE VIOLIN.

SCENE, *A hill-top with a wayside cross.*

JOHAN.

Sing sweet, sing sweet, my violin, sing ;
Sing all thy best, — sing sweet, sing sweet ;
Gay welcomes fling more swift **to bring**
The cadence of her loitering feet.
Ring strong along thy bounding wires
A song shall throng with youth's desires.
Let the yearning joy-notes linger
'Neath the coy, caressing finger,
Till the swift bow, flitting over,
Dainty as **a** doubtful **lover,**
Slyly, shyly, kisses dreaming,
Falters o'er the trembling strings,   .
And the love-tones, slower streaming,
Fade to fitful murmurings.

Another year !   Ah, fate is hard !
Another year !   My hands are scarred
With rugged toil.   The tender skill

With which they wrought my music's will
Fails as the days go by ; and yet
No term to misery is set.
Thou gentle conjurer of sound,
The one fast friend my life has found,
Vain all thy art ; though I can wing
The love-larks from each leaping string,
And heavenward send them carolling ;
Bend at my will the soul in prayer,
Bid man or maid my sorrow share ;
Can stir the ferns upon the rock,
And anguish all the air with pain ;
Or, velvet-voiced, delight to mock
The fairy footfalls of the rain, —
It helps me not. — Though I have force
To thrill the forest with remorse,
Or torture sound till every air
Dark murder hisses, and despair ;
And, 'mid the harmonies that flow,
Strange discords riot 'neath the bow,
Like 'wildered fiends astray in heaven, —
Alas, alas, why was it given,
This useless power? My wasted art
Serves but to wring a peasant's heart.

ELSA.

My Johan, have you waited long?
I heard your viol's happy song ;
I heard it call, " Come quick, come fast !"

As o'er the stepping-stones I passed.
I heard it calling, " Sweet, come fleet ! "
As up I came among the wheat.
The birds o'erhead called, " Soon, — come soon ! "
I think they know its pretty tune.
What, sad again, and ever sad ?
Play, Johan, play !   'T is eventide ;
The bells ring out the story glad
How came her joy to Mary's side.

JOHAN.

I cannot.   Better had I stayed
In yonder convent's tranquil shade,
At hopeless peace.   They meant it well
Who bade me be a priest.   The cell,
The fast, dead prayers, a palsied life,
I fought or bent to, till the strife
O'ermastered patience.   None too late
I fled beyond their cursèd gate ;
And free was I as birds are free
To fly, and yet at liberty,
Like them, to quench no single note
That trembles in the eager throat.
What slavery sweet to feel within
The song which not to sing is sin !
If He at whose divine decree
These hands interpret Him can be
So careless of the gift He gave,
What has He left me but the grave?

I plough, I dig ; far through the years
I see myself the slave of tears, —
I that have dreamed of love and fame,
A village boor, without a name.
Last week the young duke opened wide,
To please the poor, his garden's pride.
There, wandering, I saw withal
The nectarines rotting on the wall,
The tumbling grapes caught up with thread,
The dead-ripe figs hung overhead,
The fattening peaches swung in nets.
What woman's starving baby gets
One half the care that saves these pets?
Sharp, sharp the lesson. Break, sad heart,
Or learn to know the poor man's art, —
The art to bear with patience meek
The blow upon the other cheek.
How shall I bear it? I could steal,
Cheat, for this chance. You only feel,
And you alone, how hard the toil
That bends me o'er the silent soil,
And you alone what wild desires
Await a larger life ; what fires
Of wordless anguish burn unguessed,
To think, — be sure, — that unexpressed, —
A serf, a boor, — my soul has here
A gift the waiting world holds dear.
Old violin, comrade of the hours
That labour spares, what music-flowers,

What whispers wild, what visions bright,
Thy friendship brings the tired night !
And yet, like one who, sick with sin,
Would murder love he cannot win,
Twice on the bridge, at night, I stood,
To cast thee in the wrecking flood.
But when a last farewell I sung
Too stern a pang my bosom wrung ;
I could not drown the dreams that crave
Expression's life.   Best were the grave.

ELSA.

Yet that were sin !   Could I but give
My life to help your art to live !
The Alp-horn calls ; I cannot stay.
One kiss.   Ah, Johan, wait and pray.
                                    [*She sees a purse in the road.*

A purse !

JOHAN.

I pray it be not thin.

ELSA.

Nay, touch it not.   It lies within
The shadow of the cross.[8]   'T is sin.
Who taketh but a flower or stone
Where that holy shade is thrown
Is cursed to death.   His dearest prayer,
Fluttering like a prisoned bird,

Never wins the happy air,
Beats against the painted saints,
At the altar hopeless faints,
Never, never to be heard.

JOHAN.

The ban is off, — the sun is on.
St. George ! 't is full ; my luck has won.
Good thirty ducats, gold beside !
Ho for my love, my art, my bride !

ELSA.

What, take at will another's gold,
For love, for greed ?   Stay, Johan, — hold !
The duke has guests !   You cannot soil
Your soul with this.

JOHAN.

        And did they toil
To win this money ?   Out of earth
Some swarthy bondsman wrought its birth.
His sweat, his pain, to be at last
A wanton's wage, a gambler's cast !
Mine is it now to better end.

ELSA.

You cannot keep it.   Johan, friend,
A curse is on it.   Curses stay.
For gain did one Lord Christ betray :

When Satan gives another's gold,
So much of the Christ is sold.
Blessings come and heavenward go,
Wing-clipped curses bide below.
Thirty ducats, broad and bright, —
Hide them, Johan, out of sight.
Silver white, it fetcheth blight !
Gold, gold, is wicked, bold !
Hear now the story mother told :
Since **ever I was** a little maid
Ghost-gray silver makes me afraid.

Zillah's son, great Tubal Cain,
Deep he diggèd in the earth,
Where strong iron hath its birth,
Till the hurt earth sobbed with pain.
Little recked he, Tubal Cain.
The sword and the ploughshare
Out of iron he forged with care ;
Brass and copper red he found
In their coffins underground.
Then Lord Satan hired he
To dig to all eternity.
Tore he from the broken mould
Moon-white silver, sun-red gold.
On the blessèd Sabbath morn,
Tubal Cain, with laugh and scorn,
Tortured from the silver white
Thirty pieces, broad and bright.

Quick were they and sore to keep ;
None who had them gathered sleep.
Little Joseph's brethren said
They would dye his garments red ;
Thirty coins of Tubal Cain
Gat they for their brother's pain.
At the holy city's gate
Joseph and Mary long did wait ;
Neither corn nor gold had they
The cruel Roman tax to pay.
Little babe Jesu spake aloud, —
Marvelled greatly all the crowd, —
Spake the child in Mary's ear,
" Dig in the sand, and have no fear."
Deep they delved, and brought to light
Thirty pieces, broad and bright.
Foul-faced Judas sold his Lord
For to have this devil-hoard ;
Black-faced Judas had for **gain**
The thirty coins of Tubal Cain.
On the floor the coins he spent,
Brake his heart, and out he went.
All the way adown the hill
Rolled the ducats with him still ;
Underneath his gallows tree
Danced the ducats for to see.
Now they pay for murder done,
Now by them the thief is won.
Mary, Mother, and every saint

Keep me from the silver taint !
My heart from wrong, my body from pain,
My soul from sin like Tubal Cain ! [4]

JOHAN.

The purse is mine ! No old monk's tale
Shall stay my hand. If this should fail —
All men own death. How shall it be ?

ELSA.

Give me the purse ! **The purse** or me ?
Am I so little worth ?

JOHAN.

Take care ;
I hear a horse.

Enter horseman.

HORSEMAN.

Ho, fellow, there !
Hast seen a purse ? Just here it lay.

ELSA.

My Johan found it.

HORSEMAN (*takes it*).

Thanks. Good-day.
[*Rides away as a gentleman comes behind them, hidden
by the hedge.*

JOHAN.

Now is life over.

ELSA.

Never less.
Your soul is saved. Now, Johan, guess
A secret. No? Well, at the fair
Last week I sold, I pledged my hair.
To-morrow I shall fetch the gold
To win your way. Ah, love is bold.
My father? Think you I shall care?
A little hurt ; less ill to bear
Than that worse hurt you bade me share.

JOHAN.

Forgive, forget ! Ah, not again
Your trust shall fail.

ELSA.

Just one more kiss ;
And ere your sinless face I miss,
Take up the viol. Say not nay.
The twilight song. Play, Johan, play
The song that in the stillness brings
My troubled soul from earthly things,
When the blown horns the cattle call
Back to the shelter of the stall.

JOHAN.

Come home, come home.
Not through the sallow wheat,
Come home, come home,
Though to grass-tangled feet
The dewy ways be sweet.
Come home, come home,
Meek eyes and skins of silk,
Come home, come home.
Fetch the clover-scented milk,
Come home, come home.
With their pails the maidens wait,
Ever singing at the gate,
Come home, come home.
Come ye home to Mary's wings,
Joy to earth the angel rings,
Come home, come home.
Bring your load of care and sin,
Lo, she waits to let you in,
Come home, come home.

Stay, stay awhile.　Though dear my art,
More dear your love.　The tears that start
I know are joy.　Lo, Seraph wings
Flutter o'er the praying strings.
Hear the gladness of your soul
All the raptured viol thrill ;
Viewless hands my touch control,
Other force than earthly will.
Purer than the chant of saints

Rings the anthem of your heart ;
Though upon your lip it faints,
Though the tears your eyelids part,
Angel voices, pure and strong,
Catch the sweetness of the song.
Hark ! the silver crash of cymbals ;
Hear the joyous clash of timbrels,
Pouring through the shadows dim ;
All the air is music-riven,
And the organ's stately hymn
Thunders to the vault of heaven.
Murmurs, whispers, sad, mysterious,
Language of another sphere,
Faint and solemn, tender, serious,
Wander to my listening ear.

Enter gentleman.

GENTLEMAN.

A poet-lover !   Did you find my purse ?

JOHAN.

Ay; and had kept it, too, — or worse, —
Except for her.

GENTLEMAN.

      Would Eve had stayed
As honest as your blushing maid !
I always thought the story queer,
Would like that poor snake's tale to hear.

Sometimes I fancy Madam Eve
Tempted the Tempter to deceive.
I heard you tell a pretty tale
About some yellow hair for sale.
Will sell it now!   Say, gold for gold!
Let's see the goods.   [*Pulls out the comb.*
                    'T is worth, well sold,
A hundred ducats.

JOHAN.

                    No, my lord,
'T is not for sale.   No miser's hoard
Could buy it.

GENTLEMAN.

                    Say two hundred, then ;
A kiss to boot.   I know of men
Would ask for six.

ELSA.

                    'T is yours, — 't was mine !

GENTLEMAN.

Keep gold, keep hair.   Too proudly shine
Those locks above a heart of gold
For me to part them.   When you 're old,
And you have babes and he has fame,
Teach in their prayers the wild duke's name.
And you who thought a purse to keep,

Within that battered violin sleep —
Ah, but I heard — all wealth and power
Man craves on earth. "In some full hour,
When heaven is nearest, make for me
One golden fugue, to live and be
Remembered when the morrow's light
Is gone for us. Good-night, good-night.

4

MY CHATEAUX IN SPAIN.

Ho, joyous friend with beard of brown !
A half hour back 't was gray ;
A half hour back you wore a frown,
But now the world looks gay.
For here the mirror's courtly grace
Cheats you with a youthful face,
And here the poet clock of time
Each happy minute counts in rhyme ;
And here the roses never die,
And " Yes " is here love's sole reply.
What gladder land can any gain
Than this my noble realm of Spain ?
But come with me, for I am one
Hidalgo-born of Aragon ;
I will show you why I choose
Thus to live in Andalouse.
Across the terrace, up the stair,
Our steps shall wander to and fro
Where pensive stand the statues fair,
And murmur songs of long ago.
Or will you see my pictures old,
The landscapes hung for my delight
In window-frames of fretted gold,

Where, glowing, shines in colour bright
That Claude of mine at full of noon,
When the strong passion-throb of June
Stirs bird and leaf, and everywhere
The world is one gay love affair?
Or shall we linger, looking west,
Just when my Turner's at its best,
To watch the cold stars, one by one,
Crawl to the embers of the sun,
Whilst all the gray Sierra snows
Are ruddy with the twilight rose?
Believe me, artists there are none
Like those of mine in Aragon;
Nor painter would I care to choose
Beside the sun of Andalouse.
Or shall we part the shining leaves
My vines droop downward from the eaves,
And see, amidst the sombre pines,
The maiden take a shameless kiss?
Around his neck her white arm twines,
And still is sweet their changeless bliss.
I know she cannot aught refuse,
For that's the law in Andalouse,
And ever 'neath this happy sun
There is no sin in Aragon.
Or shall we cast yon casement wide,
And see the knights before us ride,
The charging Cid, the Moors that flee?
Grim although the battles be

That through my window-frames I see,
No death is there, nor any pain,
Because on my estates in Spain
All passions gaily run their course,
But lack the shadow-fiend remorse.
Something 't is to make one vain
Thus to be grandee of Spain ;
For the wine of Andalouse
All the world a man might lose,
Could he see what rosy shapes
Trample out my Spanish grapes,
Know how pink the feet that bruise
My gold-green grapes of Andalouse.
Ah, but if you 're not a don,
Drink no wine of Aragon.
Dreamland loves and elfin flavours,
Gay romances, fairy favours,
Moonlit mists and glad confusions,
Youth's brief mystery of delusions,
Racing, chasing, haunt the brain
Of him who drinks this wine of Spain.
Where the quarterings were won
That make of me a Spanish don
No one asks in Aragon.
Never blood of Bourbon grew
So magnificently blue ;
Blood have I that once was Dante's,
Kinsman am I of Cervantes.
Come and see what nobles fine

Make my proud ancestral line :
In my gallery set apart,
Lo where art interprets art.
Yes, you needs must like it well, —
Shakespeare's face by Raphael.
Ah, 't is very nobly done,
But that 's the air of Aragon.
He left me that which till life ends
Is surely mine, — the best of friends ;
And chiefly one, if you would know,
I love of all, Mercutio.
Velasquez ? Ay, he knew a man,
And well he drew my Puritan,
With eyes too full of heaven's light
To dream our day as aught but night.
If my soul stirs swift at wrong,
This sire made that instinct strong.
Da Vinci touched with love the face
That keeps for me young Surrey's grace.
And that, — ah, that is one to like,
My kinsman Sidney, by Vandyke.
Some words he gave, of which bereft
My life were poorer. There to left
Are they whose rills of English song
Unto my royal blood belong.
For poet, painter, priest, and lay
Went to make my Spanish clay ;
And here away in Andalouse,
Whatever mood my soul may choose,

The poet's joy, the soldier's force,
Finds for me its parent source
Where, along the pictured **wall,**
Hero voices on me call,
With the falling of the dews,
In Aragon or Andalouse,
When the mystic shadows troop,
When my fairy flowers droop,
And the joyous day is done
In Andalouse **or Aragon.**

May 27, 1888.

THE TOMBS OF THE REGICIDES.[5]

LUDLOW AND BOUGHTON.

ALONE on the vine-covered hillside,
Set gray 'gainst the ivy-clad walnuts,
Stands, sombre as Calvin, and barren
Of crucifix, altar, and picture,
The church of St. Martin.   A stranger,
I stood where the pride of its arches
Looks scorn on the Puritan's sadness.
Not prouder for Switzerland's annals
The glory of Morat or Sempach
Than these darkened tablets that tell us
How gladly for Ludlow and Boughton
She lifted the shield of protection,
How sternly she answered the summons
To render her guests to the headsman.
The parents that gave their true soul-life
Were England and Freedom.   Ah, surely
With courage and conscience they honoured
That parentage costly of sorrow,
And did the just deed and abided.
Long, long were the days that God gave them

With friendships and peace in this refuge,
Where sadly they yearned for the home-land,
And **saw their** great Oliver's England
Bowed low in the dust of dishonour.

August 19, 1888.

✕ CERVANTES.[6]

THERE are who gather with decisive power
The mantle of contentment round their souls,
And face with strange serenity the hour
Of pain, or grief, or any storm that rolls
Destruction o'er the tender joys of life.

There are who some great quest of heart or brain
Keep even-poised, whatever fate the years
May fetch to mock with lesser loss or gain,
And find brief joy in smiles, small grief in tears,
And tranquil take the hurts of human strife.

A few there be who, spendthrift heirs of mirth
Immortal, mock the insolence of fate,
And with a breath of jesting round the earth
Ripple men's cheeks with smiles, and gay, elate,
Sit ever in the sunshine of their mood.

Oh, royal master of all merry chords, `
Of every note in mirth's delightful scale,
To thee was spared no pang that earth affords,
Nor any woe of sorrow's endless tale, —
Want, prison, wounds, all that has man subdued ;

But, light of soul, as if all life were joy,
Forever armed with humour's shining mail,
True-hearted, gallant, free from scorn's alloy,
When life was beggared of its best, and frail
Grew hope, 't is said thou still wert lord of smiles.

This could I wish ; and yet it well may be
Thy heart smiled not, for wit, like fairy gold,
Mayhap won naught for him who scattered glee,
No help for him by whom the jest was told, —
The world's sad fool, whose ever-ready wiles

Rang the glad bells of laughter down the years,
And cheated pain with merry mysteries,
And from a prison cell, the twins of tears,
Sent forth his Don and Squire to win at ease
Such joy of mirth as his could never be.

Ah, who can say! His latest day of pain
Took Shakespeare's kindred soul. I trust they met
Where smiles are frequent, and the saddest gain
What earth denies, the privilege to forget
"The oppressor's wrong, the proud man's contumely."

But where he sleeps, the land which gave him birth,
And gave no more to him, its greatest child,
Knows not to-day. Some levelled heap of earth,
Some nameless stone, lies o'er him who beguiled
So many a heart from thinking on its pain.

Yet I can fancy that at morning there
The birds sing gladder, and at evening still
The peasant, resting from his day of care,
Goes joyous thence with some mysterious thrill
Of lightsome mirth, whose cause he seeks in vain.

October, 1888.

SUNSET AT SEA.

AT eve, by the Arno, a thought-king
Stood flushed with the wonder of knowing —
He first of all creatures, he only —
How still stands God's sun ; how earth ever
Trails spinning behind its swift motion
Unending forevers of sunsets.
Grew the thought through a childhood of groping,
The thought that last year was God's only ?
Did it smite, like the levin, at midnight
A brain that was darkened with thinking,
Strong, terrible, joyful, and brilliant,
A splendour that fiercely illumines
And troubles the wondering vision
With doubt of the truth it revealeth ?
Was it born as between two quick heart-throbs,
Surging up from the ever-unquestioned
To the questioning sight of the conscious,
A thought that should gather and grow, till,
Like billows an earthquake has builded,
It swept o'er the landmarks of knowledge,
And crumbled the distant horizon ?
Passed he then to the street and the market,

Giving back the 'good-evens' that greeted,
Still gentle, and childlike, and humble,
Aware not his **forehead bore** proudly
The terrible crown of the thought-king?

June, 1888.

TO THE SEA AT DAWN.

THE morn exults in new-born light
And, black athwart its gold,
The broken fragments of the night
Rock in their cradles old.

Ho, sturdy wooer of the great !
What need to mock thy power
With feeble woman-tales that prate
Of manhood's yielding hour?

The Norseland fury in us craves
To feel thy billows leap ;
Claims kinship with yon bounding waves,
Calls cousin with the deep.

The vigour of thy strident song,
Thy rhythmic marches gay,
Rang music to thy kinsmen strong
Where'er their hero way :

As when, upon the Spaniards' flight,
Was loosed thy stormiest power

For God and right and England's might,
In England's darkest hour ;

Or when across the death-watched wave
Our stern sea eagle swooped,
And where the bravest led the brave
His fierce young eaglets trooped.

O poet, lord of many a mood,
Like him of Arthur's hall,
That knight so bold in battle rude,
So soft at woman's call,

Thy vassal waves this summer morn,
Far o'er thy weary length,
Freight with the strength of sweetness born
The sweetness born of strength ;

And let them whisper love for me
By one remembered beach, —
Love stronger than thy wildest sea,
Kind as thy gentlest speech.

May 30, 1888.

SUNSET AT SEA.

ADOWN the thronged deck of the steamer
The babble of voices fails slowly,
As if unseen fingers of silence
Were laid on the lips of the speakers.
A blazon of azure-flecked crimson,
White-starred with the quick-leaping foam-jets,
Falls swift on the shuddering ocean ;
While high overhead to the zenith
Imperious splendours of scarlet
Flare strange, such as up from the darkness
That fell on Gethsemane's stillness
Rose red with the anguish of nature.[7]
Slow fadeth the colour that troubles
The soul with mysterious terror,
Till unto the sky and the waters
Is born the cool quiet of purples
That calm the stirred heart of the seer.
The peace which is past understanding,
Which only the heart can interpret,
Comes clad in the shadows of twilight
With meanings elusive and tender,
That die at the mere touch of thought, and
Are frail as the firstlings of April.

The peace which is past understanding :
Ethereal, viewless, and solemn,
Mysterious gift of the evening,
A love dew that comes, how we know not,
And freshens all life, how we wist not ;
Till down to the paling horizon
Are poured the night shadows, while ever
The huge striving bulk of the steamer
Hurls on through the dark and the ocean.

June 1, 1888.

5

FORGET–ME–NOTS.

ON THE ALBULA PASS.

THEY peep above the boulders gray,
Stand dark against the snows,
Leap modest **from** the billow's **kiss**
Gray Albula bestows.

They bend beneath the cloaking **mist**,
Crowd every open spot,
And murmur with assurance gay
One phrase, " *Forget me not.*"

The gentle chorus rises still
Unanimously sweet;
They seem to leave their quiet nooks,
And cluster round my feet.

Forget thee not ? **Yet how to learn**
The very ample art
To love an army corps of maids,
All bidding for my heart !

There **may** be who would think those eyes,
So constant and so true,

To be — forgive the daring thought —
Monotonously blue.

And then, if all these myriad lips
To but one song are set,
There might be luxury in the power
A little to forget.

No gay arithmetic of love
Could solve this puzzling sum,
Nor leave a Mormon lover aught
But resolutely dumb ;

For all historic cases fail
Before my hopeless lot,
When fifty thousand viewless tongues
Say just " *Forget me not.*"

Nor yet am I the first or last
By whom their cry is heard ;
They breathe it to the **careless wind**,
They cast it to the **bird**.

Who gave these mountain-maids their song ?
What lover's murmured thought
Unnumbered centuries ago
Their tender legend taught ?

Or was it from some wounded soul
In torture **and** despair
They learned these faint, appealing words, —
The wail of human prayer?

I know not.   Love is boundless, large ;
Past Albula's cloud-towers
A joyous shaft of sunshine falls
On me and on the flowers.

Mysterious vestals of the hill,
In pretty council met,
Pray teach me now that wiser art,
How easiest to forget.

The song is hushed, the drooping mist
Shrouds every silent form,
And thoughtful down the lonely **pass**
I move amid the storm.

July 8, 1888.

MINERVA MEDICA.

VERSES READ AT THE DINNER COMMEMORATIVE OF THE
FIFTIETH YEAR OF THE DOCTORATE OF D. HAYES
AGNEW, M. D., APRIL 6, 1888.

GOOD CHAIRMAN, BROTHERS, FRIENDS, AND GUESTS, —
    all ye who come with praise
To honour for our ancient guild a life of blameless
    days,
If from the well-worn road of toil I step aside to find
A poet's roses for the wreath your kindly wishes bind,
Be certain that their fragrance types, amid your laurel
    leaves,
The gentle love a tender heart in duty's chaplet weaves.

I can't exactly set the date, — the Chairman he will
    know, —
But it was on a chilly night, some month or two ago.
Within, the back-log warmed my toes ; without, the
    frozen rain,
Storm-driven by the angry wind, clashed on my win-
    dow-pane.
I lit a pipe, stirred up the fire, and, dry with thirst for
    knowledge,

Plunged headlong in an essay by a Fellow of the College.

But, sir, I've often seen of late that this especial thirst
Is not of all its varied forms the keenest nor the worst.

At all events, that gentleman — that pleasant College Fellow —

He must have been of all of us the juiciest and most mellow.

You ask his name, degree, **and fame;** you want to know that rare man?

It was n't you, — nor you, — nor you, — no, sir, 't was **not** the Chairman!

For minutes ten I drank of him; quenched was my ardent thirst;

Another minute, and my veins with knowledge, sir, had burst;

A moment more, my head fell back, my lazy eyelids closed,

And on my lap that Fellow's book at equal peace reposed.

Then I remembered me the night that essay first was read,

And how we thought it could n't all have come from one man's head.

At nine the College heard a snore and saw the Chairman start, —

A snore as of an actor shy rehearsing for his part.

At ten, a shameless chorus around the hall had run,

The Chairman dreamed a feeble joke, and said the noes had won.

At twelve the Treasurer fell asleep, the wakeful Censors slumbered,
The Secretary's minutes grew to hours quite unnumbered.
At six A. M. that **Fellow paused, perchance a** page to turn,
And up I got, and cried, " I move the College do adjourn l "
They did n't, sir ; they sat all day. It made my flesh to creep.
All night they sat ; — that could n't be. Goodness ! was I asleep?
Was I asleep? With less **effect** that Fellow might have tried
Codeia, Morphia, **Urethan, Chloral,** Paraldehyde.
In vain my servant called aloud, " Sir, here 's a solemn letter
To say they want a song from you, for lack of some one better.
The Chairman says his man will wait, while you sit down and write ;
He says he 's **not in any haste,** — and make it something light ;
He says you need n't vex yourself to try to be effulgent,
Because, he says, champagne enough will keep them all indulgent."
I slept — at least I think I slept — an hour by estimation,
But if I slept, I **must** have had unconscious cerebration

For on my desk, the morrow morn, I found this ordered verse;
Pray take it as you take your wife, — 'for better or
  for worse.'

A golden wedding: fifty earnest years
  This spring-tide day from that do sadly part,
When, 'mid a learned throng, one shy, grave lad,
  Half conscious, won the Mistress of our Art.

Still at his side the tranquil goddess stood,
  Unseen of men, and claimed the student boy;
Touched with her cool, sweet lips his ruddy cheek,
  And bade him follow her through grief and joy.

" Be mine," she whispered in his startled ear,
  "Be mine to-day, as Paré once was mine;
Like Hunter mine, and all who nobly won
  The fadeless honours of that shining line.

" Be mine," she said, "the calm of honest eyes,
  The steadfast forehead, and the constant soul,
Mine the firm heart on simple duty bent,
  And mine the manly gift of self-control.

" Not in my service is the harvest won
  That gilds the child of barter and of trade;
That steady hand, that ever-pitying touch,
  Not in my helping shall be thus repaid.

" But I will take you where the great have gone,
   And I will set your feet in honour's ways ;
Friends I will give, and length of crowded years,
   And crown your manhood with a nation's praise.

"These will I give, and more ; the poor man's home,
   The anguished sufferer in the clutch of pain,
The camp, the field, the long, sad, waiting ward,
   Watch for your kindly face, nor watch in vain ;

" For, as the sculptor years shall chisel deep
   The lines of pity 'neath the brow of thought,
Below your whitening hair the hurt shall read
   How well you learned what I my best have taught."

The busy footsteps of your toiling stand
   Upon the noisy century's sharp divide,
And at your side, to-night, I see her still,
   The gracious woman, strong and tender-eyed.

O stately Mistress of our sacred Art,
   Changeless and beautiful and wise and brave,
Full fifty years have gone since first your lips
   To noblest uses pledged that forehead grave.

As round the board our merry glasses rang,
   His golden-wedding chimes I heard to-night ;
We know its offspring ; lo, from sea to sea
   His pupil children bless his living light.

What be the marriage-gifts that we can give?
  What lacks **he** that on well-used years attends?
All that we have to give are his to-day, —
  Love, honour, and obedience, troops of friends.

NOTES.

NOTE 1.

I have accepted the popular version of Galileo's famous call to Rome to answer for his intellectual views. Much doubt has of late been thrown upon the received story of the peril to which his visit subjected him

Long after the period in question grave men of science held to the possibility of reviving youth, and also believed in the transmutability of metals.

NOTE 2.

Galileo, trained as a physician, used the pendulum as a measurer of the pulse, causing it to beat even time with any special pulse by raising or lowering the weight or bob. Thus the length of the pendulum became a conventional measure of the rate of the pulse. Counting it with the aid of a watch, although first used in the reign of Anne, was never common until the present century.

That "frail English boy" was William Harvey, the discoverer of the circulation of the blood.

NOTE 3.

The belief that it is sinful to touch that which the shadow of the cross falls upon is a mediæval fancy, but I cannot now recall where I have seen it mentioned.

NOTE 4.

I am indebted to Professor T. F. Crane, of Cornell University, for the strange legendary story of the thirty pieces of silver. I have, of course, taken great liberties with the old Latin version, as to which Professor Crane says : —

"The legend of the thirty pieces of silver is found only in Gottfried of Viterbo's Pantheon, a rare work reprinted in *Scriptores Rerum Germanicorum*, Ratisbon, 1726 (ed. Pistorius and Stoure). I have copied it from M. du Meril, *Poésies Populaires Latines du Moyen Age*, Paris, 1847, p. 321, also a scarce work. I do not know of any other accessible version, although the legend was copied from Gottfried by various legend-writers of the time. Where Gottfried got it I cannot tell."

NOTE 5.

The regicides buried in the church of St. Martin, at Vevey, are Boughton, Ludlow, and Phelps. The tombstones of the first two are visible. Phelps has recently been commemorated by a stone placed upon the wall by the American descendants of his family, — the Phelpses of New England and New Jersey. Ludlow and Boughton lived to a great age at Vevey, and so, also, I believe, did Phelps, of whom less is known.

NOTE 6.

Cervantes, who lost a hand at Lepanto, was for five years a prisoner in Algiers, and on his release lived a life of sad vicissitudes, dying in want on the 23d of April, 1616, the day of Shakespeare's death. Where lie the bones of the creator of Don Quixote is wholly unknown.

NOTE 7.

The belief that the sky flushed red over the closing moments of the crucifixion is another mediæval fancy, for which I can quote no authority. I think it is in the Golden Legends.

www.ingramcontent.com/pod-product-compliance
Lightning Source LLC
Chambersburg PA
CBHW031455270326
41930CB00007B/1010